THE LAST TIME WE SAW STRANGERS

POEMS

CHRISTOPHER HOPKINS

The Last Time We Saw Strangers $10.00

Poems by Christopher Hopkins
Clare Songbirds Publishing House Poetry Series
ISBN 978-1-947653-67-2

The Last Time We Saw Strangers © 2019 Christopher Hopkins
All Rights Reserved. Clare Songbirds Publishing House retains right to reprint.
Permission to reprint individual poems must be obtained from the author who owns the copyright.

Printed in the United States of America
SECOND EDITION

Clare Songbirds Publishing House Mission Statement:
Clare Songbirds Publishing House was established to provide a print forum for the creation of limited edition, fine art from poets and writers, both established and emerging. We strive to reignite and continue a tradition of quality, accessible literary arts to the national and international community of writers, and readers. Chapbook manuscripts are carefully chosen for their ability to propel the expansion of art and ideas in literary form.
We provide an accessible way to promote the art of words in order to resonate with, and impact, readers not yet familiar with the siren song of poets and writers. Clare Songbirds Publishing House espouses a singular cultural development where poetry creates community and becomes commonplace in public places.

140 Cottage Street
Auburn, New York 13021
www.ClareSongbirdspub.com

Contents

Sick, Thick or Lazy	7
Hometown Cuckoos	9
The Last Time We Saw Strangers	10
Islands	12
Drinking the Root Beer	14
God and Work	15
Simple physics	16
Tin Line	17
In the Owl-light	18
North American Butterfly	19
Iodine	20
Stray Dogs for Dinner	21
I Was a Boy of Blue Midnights	22
All the King's Horses	24
Harpoons	25
Public Open Spaces	26
The Everything of Silence	28
The Anxiety of Starlings	29
The Stranding	30
The Happiness of Sleeping Walking Men	31
Drowning of a Feather	32
Salting the Skin	33
Thanks for Kind Words	35
Chemistry in Old Photographs	36

Thank you to the editors of the following publications for printing my poems in various versions/incarnations.

"Sick, Thick or Lazy" – *The Morning Star*, 21 December 2017

"The Anxiety of Starlings" – *The Paragon Journal*, 5 November 2017

"Drinking the Root Beer" – *The Blue Nib Magazine*, Issue 22, 5 February 2018

"God and Work" – *Dissident Voice*, 11 March 2018

"Hometown Cuckoos" – *Riggwelter,* Issue 12, 21 August 2018

"Iodine" – *Tilde: A Literal Journa*l, Issue #1 23 March 2018

"Stray Dogs for Dinner" – *The Paragon Journal*, 7 November 2017

"Simple Physics" – *Please Hear What I'm Not Saying*. MIND anthology, February 2018

"Public Open Spaces" – *The Paragon Journal*, 10 November 2017

"The Everything of Silence – *The Paragon Journal*, 5 November 2017

"The Stranding" (Whale poem) – *The Blue Nib Magazine*, Issue 22, 5 February 2018

Tin Line – *Tuck Magazine,* 28 March 2018

"Chemistry in Old Photographs" – *Tuck Magazine,* 28 March 2018

"The Last Time We Saw Strangers" – *Tuck Magazine,* 28 March 2018

"Salting the Skin" – *Ink, Sweat & Tears*, 26 April 2018

"Drowning of a Feather" - *The Indianapolis Review*, May 2018

"North American Butterfly" – *Mojave River Review*, May 2018

"Public Open Spaces" – *The Cortland Review*, #issue 79, 3rd June 2018

For my daughter, Robyn

Sick, Thick or Lazy

There are heart-shaped marks
found in every town, saved away
in safe places, hiding
in plain view
from eyes not looking.

Spaces in heaven
where only the lights of the town
fit to the crooked shape.

Others are carved
in fingernail-deep Roman,
spelling out a familiar name.

For our fierce boy
it was a thousand steps up Penywern Hill,

a blood moon rinsed
to the black hills mourned.

He took his heart out of his chest
and planted it in the earth.

Then left
to look for work.

Hometown Cuckoos

I do wonder
how it would be
if we stayed,

settled into the corner of an old nest.
Patch its holes with dry mosses
picked in the long arms
of a sun-late afternoon.

Or would bad luck
be a rain dove
calling in on its own ghosts of happiness.

Finding us there,
where her fledglings warmed,
learnt silhouettes
                with eyes blind closed.

We'll tell her 'a feather is a feather'
and sit there in the light where she mothered into,
                and hope she'll fly away.

What would we dream of
up in our quiet orchard line,
spying for the darker outlines
on the star map scatter.

I'll ask *'should we be afraid?'*
And then you'll say to me
again,

'Its was never the shadows.
    It was the moonlight that chased us from home.'

The Last Time We Saw Strangers

The forecast ran
off the cold-starred hills
in ice-cold streams.
The Atlantic
left her snows
as the fox kill feathered leas.

We watch the moorhens land,
duck their coot heads
in flashes of red
into the flow of the umber spill, thick
with the chill.

Walking the towpath,
dressed as December, feeling with
our feet the puddle ice
bend
and give.

You kiss the sun through the strobing trees,
but I am thankful
for your kisses,
and the graffiti
on the underpass
is in a dreaming of spring,
deep
in the pale reed colours.

We move, with hitching hands
tight and bare
against the cold.
We talk of the wood-burning,
sing of the bitter peat sting,
we'll let the stale air out,
and let the goodness in.

Off the idle haul road we come,
and through the corkscrew rubus lines
we see the town's bull colours.

The last time our eyes caught with strangers,
theirs danced aside with shyness, as fleeting
as the olive-black birds.

Islands

*My promise to the ghosts has brought me home,
to my fields of a boy. My frontiers,*
    my islands of play
        are gone.
The impossible blue
turned from the golden to the common stars I could name
    and I travelled on its turning,
        lived   in its distance.
When the rain fell
from a crack in the blackbird's shell
        it fell as white fire,
      spitting off the whale crest of bedrock on the hill,
      soaking in the black rye of summer,
it was the only thing   that wished life   on the crab apple trees.
If you grew up near the church
    you would play in the long grasses of its graveside.
If you grew up on the mountain
    you would play on its edge,
      spinning with the candle-flies of town,
        and be careful of your step
        amongst the whites of its fog.

*The luster of my ghosts
has found me a bowl of wood ash*   *where to set
    these flowers that never bloom,*
while life-lines hide   on unwashed hands,
 my bound palms   softly bruise
        from the welcome cup of my fathers.
   See   how the love-lines   are around the eyes and mouth,
    like the ambush sun through the bitten trees,
      they are born on the stomach
      and worn   on the hips of our mothers,

that much   hasn't changed in fortune telling.
       Then cut me through the middle,
see my acid of life   like stacking dolls   of mother and
father,
      and mother and father.
I have this land within me,   retreated
between marrow and the bone,
and although I have chewed on my cord so often
to somehow   rid me of legends   or   on a day
      where I forget the name for *heart,*
I see the sky is brightest
                  in the western arch   to home.

Drinking the Root Beer

We spent summers picking the shells
and rust apart with points of knives,
found the devil where the earth had broke,
set eyes
on more than one horizon in a day,
and here we are,
our feet in a coolness of remembering,
a long way
from the sea.

We've inched away from outside.
Edged out the nonage boys,
became the distant
where horizons pale.
Now our wildering eyes at
youth's flawless longings.

We lived in contrasts,
between the bookends of meadow and islands.
Skying the glorious, talked down the god of the sea.
Our skin knew the dirt and sky kisses,
how we were grazed raw
under the sunlight's blessing.
How we knew just by looking.

Now we are grown.
Roots in the soils of other towns
a weave of sadness worn in a circlet of frowns.
Twenty years try to claw its way out
from depths of our laugh lines.
Each asking the other,
how did the mountain whittle down to a man?

God and Work

We have a habit of stoning prophets from time to time,
here in Jerusalem,
along the spine where weight and time deposit,
the heritage of winter's long union.

You see,
our God is a jealous god,
sunk into the language, its heart and bone,
with Jesus trapped in short stories of good
weighed down by scree of the hearthstone.

In the coiled dream, our redundant destinies,
how strong hands build these nothings of today.
How we bathe in the blame of old devilry,
as our streets became the blooded prey.

In the reliquiae of our history,
the chapel at its heart stands empty.

Simple Physics

Are cormorants born with the theory of refraction
or do they learn to hunt
by mirrors?

How you see around corners
through your tears
always makes me feel
that child-like wonder.

There have been day when oceans have been
dripping off my wings,
my stomach singing tunes.

Then I was fed by you.

I traced a map to our house on your back
while you felt my gravity pull through you.

I shall not be afraid when I am lost.
I shall not   be afraid   when I   am lost.

I hear there are some good theories on
why we talk about love,
when the world needs our gratitude,
when the world is burning some streets along,

making the sunset sweeter,
when the words shoal for feeding.

Tin Line

I watch the buffalos from the train.
Catch the nervous shiver twitch
in their shoulders as they line.
The thick cold breath
calls up all the cherub robes,
up from this herd of gas cans
on the road, up
to the lack of imagination of a sky
grieving over the junction.

I see the air-dancers in the car lots
moving like Israel in the shallows.
Line upon line of
the fly belly colours
where the tents go back to back.
There I feel the bend and judder sway,
fighting the capsize,
the muffled steel rhyme, the hypnosis
in symphony of pressure hits
and doppler shifts which mark
the landscape passing.
The sound wave of the city
building by the mile.

I lean into my untameable portrait.
Locked in the stare of my exile eyes,
talking lockjaw to my next to kin,
brimming
with magnolia blush
waiting for the straphanger rush and heave,
wide awake
with the birds in the station rafters.
We scatter, like wheel-spit
seeds into the city.
And as our unspeaking family
we'll all ride the dry pod home.

In the Owl-light

The sheets don't show the dirt at night.
The night soaks up the blood.

I would keep the windows open in the day
but the air never really changed,

      the smell of the unwashed after the rain.

In the owl-light,
the long grass out front
hides my feet like brook water
and the wetness is as pure.

I feed the dog ham and sleep my weekend,
I dream of the bus seat emptiness
and I wake as the helpless boy
with the ghost town stomach,

      wondering at 5am.

All the *Good Morning* sighs of a punch card life.
I tidy myself up
              and smile as wide as the wolf.

North American Butterfly

Beauty is a wave,
like radio out near Jupiter
singing to the storm.
Maybe I see these things as fire,
waiting.
Maybe I should call them
today's miracle.
No one asks the Sun where it has been
rinsing its hands on the newness of a day.
The birds have lost their voice,
whether they sing for love or loss
they soon called it off and settled
in to the lessen shade.
There're rumours out west
that the orchards still give fruit,
while our rooflines bask in gasoline.
Under the shade of chaos
feeding on a split mango,
in the collage of butterfly wings,
I find my first of the day.
My jewelled wave.
My second is in ricochet.
The echo of running feet,
the hard pings off concrete.
Sound has no horizon
and is nothing without perspective.
I never questioned their haste.
I catch only the flow
of a new accent in passing,
only a divine flash of a tender sun
off the wall of a mirrorball valley,
a god blinding me to riches
& to the dolour signs
running through its rill.
In the young dusk
where the starlight stops,
I'll still say the *sky is blue*
when ever I am asked.

Iodine

After a driest day blue, an iodine smear,
low and seen with rolling eyes.
The long grasses could be called weeds for hiding our sins.
See the crows feet of the pumpkin through the river trees.
The Tycho gasp
but he never looks away.
An engine roll
as a Shepard tone approaching.
Headlights searching fingers
through the bracken line
but we are not found,
burning bright.
The night pulls over
loosely as our blanket,
bodies moist before the dew.
The stars shone on our limbs
on our lilac pale skins.
We fell into the wells
of our eight-ball eyes.

Stray Dogs For Dinner

We missed the first frosts
in warm unmade beds.
That scent was us.

The sun was low
and in the room with us all day,
over the arms of chairs and
up against the walls,
the warmth made the shape
of your back.

It sleeked around us all afternoon
and walked out the door by four.

Us, stray dogs for dinner.
Pack animals holding hands.
Raw cheeked,
warm lipped and
blood up from the run.
A night and day
and a night to come.
All alight
inside the other.

Our love,
not yet ready
for housebreaking.

I Was a Boy of Blue Midnights

In my jaw-bone youth,
I'd watched the great stone drift from the blackened lush.
I could see how the night slid on its fault-lines
        into day.

My late hours
were not wasted in life dreaming-absence.
My dreaming would run with a wolf heart in its mouth
and up the necks of the flowering vision,
        as I was a boy of blue midnights,

in nights
of electric easy
on warm dimpling perfect skin,
        scalding in our youth,
              making our fortunes on the bodies of others
                      to tip toes farewells of early hours.

That walk in light,

that walk in golden light,
when only the morning moon knows my happy trail
        and drivers in the passing cars
            who reminisce on watching me,
                on their youthful openings in single
                beds,
        of their soft conquests of happiness.

On watching me,
remembering the windfall names
on the tips of wet tongues and teeth of beer,
those mornings
where the sun puts the colour back in their hair,
plucked white by the thieves of being,
how love's short longings had long been fed to age's fire,

      the burning of hopeful touches,
      and the last drops of the hour glass sands drop,
          piling high on pillows
              to be turned again on love, love, my
              love.

I was a boy of blue midnights and a man
in the threads of gold mornings.

All the King's Horses

For shipwrecked hearts
that bask in love's smugglers' light
there's a darkness we don't understand.

The dark things call themselves luck.
But it doesn't feel as luck.
Luck should feel of happiness,
the shine of starlight
to the arms of lovers
and their tumid lips.

Not relief
not lit by a fervid glare.

I feel the ache in the heart
and the liver.
Love's path of blood and brain.
How its written in the DNA.
How the cancer in the stomach
ends up in the brain.

Promise me one thing my love.
Put me back together at the end.

Harpoons

The glaze of *Ocean Fresh*
comes through the hand wide ajar.
Our cotton husks tumbled in wreckage.
The nylon brand light has opened the bed,
whittling my bones into the shapes
of whales and harpoon heads.
I turn with the tide
in my stomach
and the white crag in my head.

We have feasted in this soap of this weekend,
pulled the rib bone of work days
from our throats.

I breathe. I effect

only in a shiver wave
in the finest of your hairs,
as if your unconscious eye
still guards you
against the presence of a wolf
and then is as quick to feel
its own kind in the den.

Lost is the feeling of separation.
To connect,
like the earth and stars joined by a burning stone.
How the heaven threw a rock at our paper scissors
and we called it love.
How we have swallowed it in each other.

I let my finger tips brush off
the star dust
onto the sheets.

Public Open Spaces

When the light comes   with a winter's morning
when even the evergreens hold their breath
and the sugar kicks wait   while the children are sleeping

that light
pouring in

the stop motion thaw   lowering the shadows back to the
earth

into the kingdoms of the dormant borders

the line   mass and colour
anchored   to the earth's bare lead.

Unhiding sweet wrappers
lay unsettling to the eye

as the calf carcass of a lightening strike's dead.
Striped   bleached

between the rods of iron roses

as dying frescos   of an old season's dare.

A flattened coke can wreath
laid at the foot   of the oak bough

in an act of remembrance   to the young summer bodies
fallen
on the cooling pear lawns.

Tarmac rivers along the side
confuse the swans every now and then

and the only way the memorial stones will move anymore
is when the mammoths return.

And there, on the park bench uprights   nailed brass
plaques
flicker to life the dead names of the loved
who found their escape in this view

who sat and watched over their healing turf.
Or maybe it was the sun-bathing limbs of June.

The Everything of Silence

Even the crows are bored with today.
The park benches never lost their damp,
the timbers of sunken ships
stacked against the pathway.

Lunch time doesn't even break
the everything of silence,
The idleness of a day
not paying attention.

Colour doesn't work today.
The cars and the post boxes
aren't red at all,
and the grass is greasy and thin.

Desire lines are skipped,
or the telling mud on leather
while our shadows stay home
waiting for the sun

to stir the wasps
amongst the pomegranate trees.
To wish our lives
so very far away.

The Anxiety of Starlings

There is a wonder
to the anxiety of the starlings.
Oiled
and starved.
How beauty can fall out of something.
How their shiver made a whale.
The sky-dance of a fattening shadow.
Round and full,
stretched and curve.
They are the pitch and duration
on the stave of power lines,
the supersonic candy floss
stretching from the coral birth.
The fluxing crown
above the cut slate town,
the church's black dagger
and the lakes of the carpark spaces.
A drowning chorus
of a hundred thousand frightened mouths.
The dance of our ghost,
in a solid state.

The Stranding

We don't hear the inconsolable whale
as we try to push it back to the sea.

It whispers its prayers
in monotone lip,
to try and make its god
bored with its dreaming.
But still it kicks.

Did the whale swim
in straight line to the shore
or happen upon a drowning,

away from the screams in the breakers,
far from the teasing witches
sea weed fingers
as it tries to dry its tears
once again.

The Happiness of Sleepwalking Men

I
let my dream stir
with the furthest branches, circle rush,

let my dreaming swim
out of the guard of the sickle-bay moon
and into the drink of the deep han blue,

where the god spit stars
were nothing more than
holes for me to breathe.
No more than a fabric nick
from the cherub's teeth,
where the day goes to find its leave.

There   was
                nothing more to
                              see.

Drowning of a Feather

The feather wind.
Hard enough fighting gravity
to be caught by water,
binding colour and barb.

Little boat of oblivion.

I am soaked in life,
scotched tight by the life giving.
Thinking this plash
is the start of an ocean.
The streetlight major,
the burnt wings on the serpent.

Salting the Skin

The sea becomes the colour of whale skin & chalk.
Hanging on a day
abandoned by the chalk light.

The worm moon
left its portrait under a drifting ebb,
sketched in ridges
by the salt water swirls
and the endless boxing sands.
I am looking out,
with the land behind me
where the oil works shimmers
in its nightly crown,
like every swallowed light of the ocean
speared to the ground.
The compact black of the
sea in front of me,
this black hole of quiet gravity.

I am the only light on the ocean.

Then a false phare beam
breaks the hill brow to my side.
Car lights strands me as the whale,
sunk in the sour-dunes
of dreaming.
Every tear,
salting the skin to crack,
under stresses,
under duress of my hidden moons,
my own careless forces of gravity.
Like the face of the tracer moon
I see my light
to be hung
on the broken starry.

Thanks for Kind Words

Night colours twist their loom
'round the star white sheer.
All clean, all bright,
'though eyes are set benighted.

Walking the room, divining for smiles
with those who shared in prayer,
who sung a gentle starry hymn,
their pale voices thin.

The cherry wood fell with a sense of steer
and varnish sealed its dreaming grain.
The endurance of the body,
an innocent feign.

We thanked each one for their kind words,
sink holes rimmed
in every line,
stumbling with embraced goodbyes.

The breast doesn't stop its giving,
and the ache of the womb
is the black of the ribbon.

Chemistry in Old Photographs

There is a truth in old photos
a certain light of green halos.
How the chemistry fading in colours is a measure
of how faraway there has become.

Mam, Dad, Home.

We ache of love in our pasts.
How these things dig into us,
break our surface with the force
of root joints splits the asphalt.

These un—coded moments,
my oddments of shelter,
are filled only with the sunlight's shadow.
We all wore the same plaid shirts.
Young skins held by the new mother.
The harvest yellow kitchen.
Awkward in the lap of some old loved ghost,
in those red backed chairs,
which could smoke a room in seconds like fires could.

We look now
knowing where the blood goes,
how the year ends.

The photo was the physical.
It was the effort, the commitment.
Our butterfly nets above the flux of life,
a front door to our permanence
of such a fleeting thing.
Here, everything stops growing,
our tailored cut to memory.
My veins are flat against the paper,
the hard and the sunlight flash.

We need the physical,
the chemistry.

.

Christopher Hopkins was born and raised in Neath, South Wales. He currently resides in the Canterbury area of Kent with his wife and daughter.

His debut poetry chapbook 'Take Your Journeys Home' was published by Clare Songbirds Publishing House in November 2017 and has received a nomination for the IPPY book award for poetry and two of its poems 'Sorrow on the Hill' and 'Smoke and Whiskey' have also received nominations for the Pushcart Prize.

Christopher has had poems published in The Morning Star, Tilde, Backlash Press, Riggwelter Press, The Paragon Journal, Ink Sweat & Tears, Indianapolis Review, Mojave River Review, The Blue Nib Magazine, Ibis Head Review, The Journal (formally the Contemporary Anglo – Scandinavian poetry), Rust & Moth, Harbinger Asylum, Scarlet Leaf Review, Anti-Heroin Chic, VerseWrights, Tuck Magazine, Dissident Voice magazine, Poetry Superhighway, Duane's PoeTree, Outlaw Poetry.

His spoken word poetry has also featured in a podcast of Golden Walkmen Magazine podcast, which also is to be included for their 'Best of the Year'. Christopher also has had work feature in the MIND Anthology called 'Please Hear What I'm Not Saying' (February 2018). Christopher also has a YouTube channel dedicated to his poetry readings.